# THE FABULOUS LOST & FOUND

## AND THE LITTLE GREEK MOUSE

WRITTEN BY MARK PALLIS
ILLUSTRATED BY PETER BAYNTON

NEU WESTEND
— PRESS —

For Alkisti, Fairuz & Phaedra - MP

For Hannah and Skye - PB

First Printing, 2020
ISBN: 978-1-9160801-9-5
NeuWestendPress.com

# THE FABULOUS LOST & FOUND

## AND THE LITTLE GREEK MOUSE

WRITTEN BY MARK PALLIS
ILLUSTRATED BY PETER BAYNTON

NEU WESTEND
— PRESS —

In the middle of the big city is a tiny yellow building. If anyone loses anything, this is where it ends up.

It is called the Lost and Found.

Mr and Mrs Frog keep everything
safe, hoping that someday every lost
watch and bag and phone and toy
and shoe and cheesegrater will find
its owner again.

But the shop is very small. And
there are so many lost things. It
is all quite a squeeze, but still, it's
fabulous.

One sunny day, a little mouse walked in.

"Welcome," said Mrs Frog. "What have you lost?"

"Έχω χάσει το καπέλο μου," said the mouse.

Mr and Mrs Frog could not speak Greek. They had no idea what the little mouse was saying.

*What shall we do?* they wondered.

*Maybe she's lost an umbrella. Everyone loses an umbrella at least twice,* thought Mr Frog.

"Have you lost this?" asked Mr Frog.

"Μία ομπρέλα; Όχι," replied the mouse.

Then Mrs Frog remembered something
that had been handed in a few months ago...

"Is this yours?" Mrs Frog asked, holding up a chunk of cheese.

"Τυρί; Όχι. Βρωμάει!" said the mouse.

"Time to put that cheese in the bin dear," said Mr Frog.

"Maybe the word 'καπέλο' means coat," said Mr Frog.

"Now where did I put that nice
yellow one?"

"Got it!" said Mr Frog.

"Ένα παλτό; Όχι. Έχω χάσει το καπέλο μου," said the mouse.

She was starting to feel a bit frustrated.

"We need to keep trying," said Mrs Frog.

Δεν είναι κασκόλ.

Δεν είναι παντελόνι.

Δεν είναι φούτερ.

Δεν είναι γυαλιά ηλίου.

Ούτε παπούτσια.

"Έχω χάσει το καπέλο μου,"
said the mouse.

Δεν είναι δύο ποδήλατα.

Δεν είναι υπολογιστής.

Δεν είναι τρία βιβλία.

Ούτε τέσσερις μπανάνες.

Ούτε πέντε κλειδιά.

It was no good. A fat wet tear rolled
down the mouse's cheek.

"How about a nice cup of tea?" asked Mrs Frog kindly.

"Λατρεύω το τσάι. Ευχαριστώ," replied the mouse. They sat together, sipping their tea and all feeling a bit sad.

Suddenly, the mouse realised she could try pointing.

She pointed at her head.
"Καπέλο!" she said.

"I've got it!" exclaimed Mrs Frog, leaping up.

"A wig of course!" said Mrs Frog.

"Δεν είναι περούκα," said the mouse.

Δεν είναι κόκκινη.

Δεν είναι ξανθιά.

Δεν είναι καφέ.

Δεν είναι πράσινη.

Δεν είναι πολύχρωμη.

"What about this?"
asked Mr Frog, pulling back
a curtain.

"Καπέλο!" exclaimed
the mouse.

"Ah, so 'καπέλο' means hat.
Wonderful!" Mr and Mrs
Frog cheered.

Πολύ ψηλό.

Πολύ μικρό.

Πολύ μεγάλο.

Πολύ σφιχτό.

"One hat left," said
Mrs Frog, reaching all
the way to the back of the
cupboard.

"It couldn't be this
old thing, could it?"

"Το καπέλο μου.

Βρήκα το καπέλο μου!

Ευχαριστώ πολύ," said the mouse.

And just like that, the mouse found her hat.

"Αντίο," she said, as she skipped away.
"Αντίο," replied Mr and Mrs Frog.

"I wonder who will come tomorrow?" said Mr Frog.
Mrs Frog put her arm around him.

"I don't know," she replied, giving him a squeeze.
"But whoever it is, we'll do our best to help."

## LEARNING TO LOVE LANGUAGES

An additional language opens a child's mind, broadens their horizons and enriches their emotional life. Research has shown that the time between a child's birth and their sixth or seventh birthday is a "golden period" when they are most receptive to new languages. This is because they have an in-built ability to distinguish the sounds they hear and make sense of them. The Story-powered Language Learning Method taps into these natural abilities.

## HOW THE STORY-POWERED LANGUAGE LEARNING METHOD WORKS

We create an emotionally engaging and funny story for children and adults to enjoy together, just like any other picture book. Studies show that social interaction, like enjoying a book together, is critical in language learning.

Through the story, we introduce a relatable character who speaks only in the new language. This helps build empathy and a positive attitude towards people who speak different languages. These are both important aspects in laying the foundations for lasting language acquisition in a child's life.

As the story progresses, the child naturally works with the characters to discover the meanings of a wide range of fun new words. Strategic use of humour ensures that this subconscious learning is rewarded with laughter; the child feels good and the first seeds of a lifelong love of languages are sown.

**For more information and free downloads visit www.neuwestendpress.com**

# ALL THE BEAUTIFUL GREEK WORDS AND PHRASES FROM OUR STORY

| | |
|---|---|
| Έχω χάσει το καπέλο μου | I've lost my hat |
| Μία ομπρέλα | an umbrella |
| Τυρί | cheese |
| Βρωμάει | it stinks |
| παλτό | coat |
| κασκόλ | scarf |
| παντελόνι | trousers |
| γυαλιά ηλίου | sunglasses |
| φούτερ | jumper |
| παπούτσια | shoes |
| ένας | one |
| δύο | two |
| τρία | three |
| τέσσερις | four |
| πέντε | five |
| υπολογιστής | computer |
| βιβλία | books |
| κλειδιά | keys |
| μπανάνες | bananas |
| ποδήλατα | bicycles |
| Λατρεύω το τσάι | I love tea |
| Ευχαριστώ | thank you |
| Ευχαριστώ πολύ | thank you very much |
| περούκα | wig |

| | |
|---|---|
| κόκκινη | red |
| ξανθιά | blond |
| καφέ | brown |
| πράσινη | green |
| πολύχρωμη | multicoloured |
| Όχι | no |
| Το καπέλο μου | my hat |
| Πολύ ψηλό | too tall |
| Πολύ μεγάλο | too big |
| Πολύ μικρό | too small |
| Πολύ σφιχτό | too tight |
| Βρήκα το καπέλο μου | I've found my hat |
| Αντίο | goodbye |

Made in the USA
Coppell, TX
11 October 2021

63890289R00021